THE
DIVISION OF
BERLIN

John Dudman

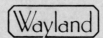
Wayland

The Arab-Israeli Issue
The Conflict in Afghanistan
The Division of Berlin
The Cuban Missile Crisis
The Hungarian Uprising
The Partition of India
The Irish Question
The Revolution in Iran
The Korean War
The Rise of Solidarity
The Crisis in South Africa
The Suez Crisis
The Vietnam War

Editor: Hazel Songhurst

First published in 1987 by
Wayland (Publishers) Ltd
61 Western Road, Hove
East Sussex BN3 1JD, England

Printed and bound in Great Britain at The Bath Press, Avon

British Library Cataloguing Publication Data
Dudman, John
    The division of Berlin.—(Flashpoints).
    1. Berlin (Germany)—Politics and
    government—1945–
    I. Title   II. Series
    943.1′55087   DD881

ISBN 1-85210-021-4

Contents

1
Imprisonment of a nation

The wall that cut Berlin in half in August 1961, runs across the city like an ugly scar symbolizing, for the first time in history, the imprisonment of a nation. The days after the Wall was built were filled with tension. At night, when the alarms sounded in East Berlin, the searchlights snapped on, illuminating the bristling barbed wire, the barriers of huge iron crosses, the shadows that could hide a runaway

seeking freedom in West Berlin only yards away. Flares released into the dark sky revealed barking alsatians running on trailing leads along the strip of no-man's land in front of the Wall. In the watch towers, guards peered through binoculars, machine guns at the ready.

Today, few East Germans seeking sanctuary in the West would dare brave the Wall: too many of their countrymen have died or fallen wounded in attempts to beat the 165 kilometre-long barrier.

The creation of the Wall was inevitable. The East German government faced an intolerable situation in the 1950s and early 1960s, when thousands of refugees fled from the realities of post-war austerity and life under communist rule in an ever-growing exodus that threatened to

East German refugees queueing to enter the West.

A woman chats to a neighbour up at a window on the opposite side of the barrier.

Opposite Soviet troops guard the border at Checkpoint Charlie as construction begins on the Wall.

wreck the economy of their country. To maintain the life of the nation, the communist leaders were forced into transforming it into a prison.

The memories of 13 August 1961 are understandably bitter for West Berliners when they recall how on that historic day they watched the Wall begin to snake across their city. As the concrete blocks were slammed into place, in the days and weeks that followed, human contact between both parts of the city was lost. And not only did the Wall divide the centre of Berlin, it continued around the perimeter of West Berlin, enclosing it in a jagged, inverted D-shaped bulwark.

From the moment the Wall began to appear, some 60,000 people living in East Berlin realized with shock that they would no longer be able to reach their offices or factories on the western side. Checkpoints were set up and manned by East German troops to block or monitor traffic trying to cross the dividing line, and East Berlin was cut off from the West.

Yet to many East Germans, the Wall became a spur to

their dreams of finding freedom. Since it went up, almost 5,000 refugees have escaped to West Berlin and democracy. More than a hundred escapees were wounded, and thousands arrested. Since 1982, however, the escapes have dwindled to a mere three or four a year, as an unknown number of freedom-seekers take holidays in East European countries without any intention of ever returning home. Since the Second World War, there has also been a trickle of refugees from West to East, most leaving their homes for ideological reasons.

Today, Berlin remains sensitive to international tension, a possible flashpoint for war, a meeting-place of East and West that has often served as an exchange point for spies. It has posed an insoluble political and diplomatic problem since it fell to the victorious Allied armies at the end of the Second World War.

On the right is Conrad Schumann, the first East German border guard to flee to the West after the Wall was built in 1961. The younger man escaped to West Berlin in 1986.

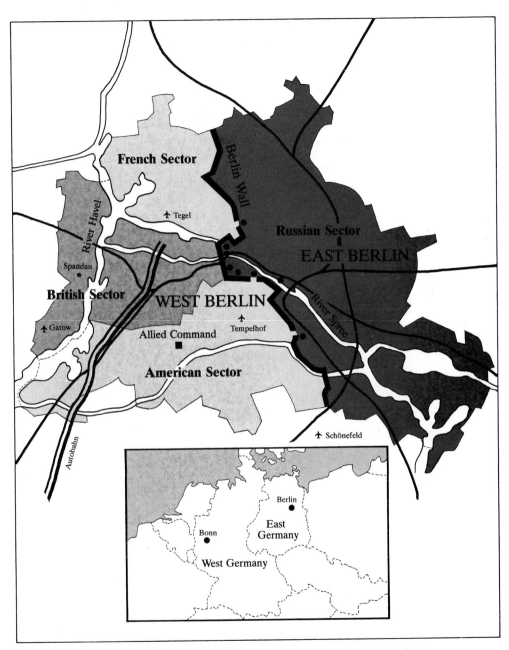

French Sector

Berlin Wall

✈ Tegel

River Havel

Russian Sector

EAST BERLIN

Spandau

British Sector

WEST BERLIN

River Spree

✈ Gatow

Allied Command ■

✈ Tempelhof

American Sector

Autobahn

✈ Schönefeld

Berlin

East
Germany

Bonn

West Germany

This map shows how Berlin is divided by the Wall, and the areas taken by the four sectors.

13

US President, John F. Kennedy's historic visit to Berlin in June 1963. His speech to the gathered crowds assured them that West Berlin would never be abandoned by the West. The mayor of West Berlin, Willy Brandt, is at far left. He later became West German Chancellor.

Under international law, the city – the largest industrial centre between Paris and Moscow – is still occupied by the four triumphant Allies: Britain, France, the USA and the Soviet Union. Two million Berliners live in the three Western Sectors and just over one million in the Soviet Sector, East Berlin, and also the capital of the German Democratic Republic.

The prime duty of the three Western nations is to defend their rights and responsibilities in West Berlin. An uneasy atmosphere has become an accepted part of life for West Berliners. Their buoyant, even optimistic, mood is seldom shaken by crises. They have learned to live with the knowledge that they are encircled by a ring of steel: 95,000 Soviet and East German troops with 1,300 tanks, a brigade of tactical nuclear weapons and more than 300 heavy artillery guns.

Their confidence is founded largely on the words of US President John F. Kennedy, speaking in Berlin on 26 June 1963. 'All free men, wherever they may live, are citizens of Berlin. And therefore, as a free man, I take pride in the words – *Ich bin ein Berliner* (I am a citizen of Berlin)'. To the West Berliners, those words were a pledge and a promise. Kennedy promised that America would never give up its responsibilities to them and their city, positioned 165 kilometres inside the East Communist bloc. To the Kremlin he signalled that Washington would never allow West Berlin to be abandoned without a fight.

How Berlin emerged from the ruin of war to become a part-communist, part-democratic enclave within the boundaries of the Soviet bloc, represents a remarkable saga in the relationship between East and West since the Second World War. Today, West Berlin has shown that it can overcome the grief of bloodshed and accept all the political contortions of those years as its population looks to the future with cautious confidence.

A present-day view of the Wall, with the slogan 'Freedom for all political prisoners in the DDR' daubed across it, and no-man's land stretching beyond it.

2
The capture of Berlin

Opposite *At dawn on 1 May 1945, Russian soldiers planted the Soviet flag on top of the Reichstag building in Berlin.*

This photograph of Hitler was taken the day the Red Army reached outer Berlin.

On 20 April 1945, Adolf Hitler's last birthday, the first Red Army troops reached the outskirts of his embattled capital, Berlin. Twelve days of bitter fighting followed. On 30 April, the Nazi dictator took his own life in his bunker beneath the State Chancellery, and two days later his troops surrendered amid the ruins. On 8 May, the final unconditional surrender of Germany was accepted by the victorious Allied armies.

17

Field Marshal Montgomery reads the terms of the German surrender to General Admiral von Friedeburg, in the left of the picture.

In Berlin itself, two million people had survived the final Red Army onslaught, and years of RAF and USAF raids that had destroyed one third of their city. But already their future had been decided by the Allies, who were determined that never again would Germany launch another war.

The first meeting of the Anglo-American-Russian European Advisory Commission to discuss the post-war division of Germany had been held at Lancaster House in London on 14 January 1944. The next day, Britain presented its plan, which placed the Soviet zone's western

Constant air raids inflicted terrible devastation on the city of Berlin.

Winston Churchill, the British prime minister, was insistent that Berlin should come under joint Allied control.

border almost exactly where it remains today, giving Russia 40 per cent of defeated Germany, and leaving Berlin marooned from the West.

One month later Russia accepted the British formula. But from the US State Department in Washington there was still no word of agreement. The high-level view was that the boundaries of future occupation zones was a military matter and not a political one. According to US officials, the zones would be determined by the location of troops at the moment of Germany's defeat. However, from the positions of the Allied armies in Europe, it was apparent that Russia would take Berlin first. The British prime minister, Winston Churchill, foresaw the implications of this, and believed it imperative that the former capital city should be under joint Allied occupation.

On 12 September 1944, the final formula for the division

of Germany was approved by all the Allies, with the description of the Soviet zone of occupation – the present-day German Democratic Republic – ending with the words '... with the exception of the Berlin area for which a special system of occupation is provided.'

This ensured that Berlin would not be part of the Soviet zone of occupation but would be taken over by the armed forces of Britain, USA and Russia. France joined as a fourth occupying power on 1 May 1945. A governing authority known as the Allied Kommandantura was set up with jurisdiction for the whole of Berlin, each power stationing troops and civic authorities in its sector.

The Four-Power administration was officially confirmed by the Churchill-Roosevelt-Stalin meeting at Potsdam in the summer of 1945, resulting in the so-called Potsdam Agreement, and put into effect.

After years of argument and disagreement between the Allies, the Four-Power presence for governing Berlin was ultimately confirmed by the Quadripartite Agreement of 1972. For the first time, Russia recognized by treaty the rights of the Western Allies in West Berlin.

The Potsdam conference held in July 1945, confirmed the Four-Power administration of Berlin, Churchill can be seen on the bottom left and, seated on the opposite side of the table is the moustached figure of Joseph Stalin.

HELMSTEDT
US ZONE
BRITISH ZONE
RUSSIAN ZONE

A British soldier checks a car and driver which have just crossed from the Russian zone of the country. The division of Germany was agreed in 1944.

The agreement also ensured that the ties between West Berlin and the Federal Republic would be maintained and developed. This confirmed the already established practice of upholding political, economic and financial links, while accepting that West Berlin remained separate from the constituent part of West Germany, and would not in future be governed by Bonn, the Federal capital. In this way, the strange position of West Berlin in relation to the Federal Republic was officially recognized and accepted. For while Bonn regards West Berlin as part of West Germany (its 11th *Land*, or province, with its own mayor) the supreme authority in the city remains with the three allied Western powers.

The agreement also confirmed that there should be un-impeded traffic on the *autobahns*, railways, air corridors, and waterways linking West Germany with West Berlin. Guaranteeing free access to West Berlin has always been the chief responsibility of the Allied powers in the city. West Berliners, also, would be allowed to cross over to East Berlin for thirty days each year, instead of the previously limited visits at Christmas, Easter and Whitsun.

In recent years, much of the tension over West Berlin has eased, but occasionally the East German authorities emphasize their control of the Berlin checkpoints. In the spring of 1986 – a few months before the twenty-fifth anniversary of the building of the Wall – they insisted that all Western diplomats should carry passports in addition to their normally accepted identity documents when crossing the boundary into East Berlin.

Britain, France and America lodged a strong protest on the grounds that the move infringed Berlin's special Four-Power status. The East Germans finally backed off, and exempted diplomats from the occupying nations, but insisted that other NATO envoys should continue to observe the regulation.

For the Allied powers in West Berlin, it was another exercise in the East German process of reminding them that the city that offers a shop window for democracy within the boundaries of communism can never be totally free from stress.

West Berliners cross to visit relatives in East Berlin during the Christmas 1965 visiting period.

23

3
The siege of Berlin

At Checkpoint Charlie during the Berlin blockade, a Soviet armoured vehicle halts in the middle of the road, and armed troops walk the streets.

The Cold War of mutual suspicion and antagonism that has so often characterized the relationship between the major powers of East and West reached crisis point in the grim days of the Berlin blockade in 1948–49.

Ernst Reuter, member of the Social Democratic Party, who was Mayor of Berlin during the crisis.

The Soviet siege was part of a Soviet plan to force Britain, America and France out of Berlin and leave the city open to a communist take-over. The crisis lasted for eleven months and ended in failure for Russia after a massive Western day-and-night airlift of food and fuel enabled the beleaguered West Berliners to survive their ordeal. But it left the city clearly divided between the democratic Western sectors, and the Russian-controlled Eastern zone, which was destined to become part of the German Democratic Republic in October, 1949, after the formation of the Federal Republic of Germany in May of the same year.

The crisis stemmed from several political developments in the immediate post-war years. In 1946, a Berlin city election held under the auspices of the controlling wartime Allies, showed a landslide victory for the *Sozialdemokratische Partei Deutchslands* (Social Democratic Party of Germany), leaving the Communist Socialist Unity Party bottom of the poll. A year later, Russia displayed its attitude to the result by vetoing the appointment of the SPD candidate, Ernst Reuter, as Lord Mayor of Greater Berlin.

After the war, too, came the problem of deciding the best course of action for Germany. The four Allies were not in agreement. The Soviet Union wanted to plunder and weaken the country and claim some reparation for its own losses. Britain and the USA wanted Germany to flourish under a stable economy and, in this way, prevent the rise of another Hitler, who had previously come to power during economic chaos. But West Germany, divided into three separate occupation zones, was an expensive burden for the Western Allies. It was agreed that a centralized financial system was necessary to ensure that West Germany prospered, and discussions on currency reform began. The failure to reach agreement on the new currency, and the proposition by Britain and the USA to merge their zones angered the Soviet Union, which had viewed the determination of the Western Allies for an independent, powerful West Germany as a threat to its own frontiers. On 5 June 1947, the US Marshall Plan (named after US Secretary of State, George Marshall) was announced. In line with US President Truman's post-war doctrine of containing communism against the threat of Soviet expansion,

The Russian delegation at an Allied Control Council meeting in 1948. Marshal Sokolovsky is third from right.

it was designed to give economic aid and relief to help rebuild the European economy and to restore strength to West Germany in particular.

Soviet distrust grew stronger and on 20 March 1948, at a meeting of the Control Council, Marshal Sokolovsky, the Soviet Commander-in-Chief, accused Britain and the USA of taking action that contravened the Potsdam Agreement and of having eliminated their right to be in Berlin at all. Finally, at the 29 May 1948 meeting of the Kommandantura, matters reached stalemate and the Soviet representatives walked out. From midnight on 18 June, the Russians began operations that stopped all traffic to the city from the West.

Immediately, Britain and the US unveiled their plan for an airlift to provide isolated West Berlin with essential supplies. At that time, food stocks were sufficient for only one month. General Clay, the US military governor, vowed: 'They cannot drive us out of Berlin by anything short of war'. He and his British counterpart, General Sir Brian Robertson, were fully prepared for the confrontation, which was to deepen, bringing Russia and the West close to war.

Men unloading sacks of flour from a US transport plane at Tempelhof airport. Planes were landing every three minutes, loaded with essential supplies.

27

On 22 June, Russia announced that the blockade was complete. From then on, the greatest airlift of modern times began, with hundreds of aircraft touching down at the British airstrip at Gatow and the American base at Tempelhof. The aerial armada built up until the skies over Berlin throbbed with the constant roar of planes flying non-stop into the city. They flew through narrow 'air corridors' at precise heights and speeds and in all weathers, arriving on a strict minute-by-minute timetable.

A 'missed' landing for the British York and Dakota aircraft, and the American 'Flying Fortresses' and Skymasters, was a calamity liable to upset the continuous flow of planes heading for Berlin. Soviet fighters sometimes 'buzzed' them, particularly any plane drifting from the recognized corridors. Inevitably, there were crashes and 65 airmen, mostly British and Americans, were killed.

In the first twenty-four hours of the airlift, 390 aircraft arrived with food and other vital supplies. Coal was ferried in, packed in thousands of kitbags. Because salt would

A British plane takes a human cargo on board during the blockade.
These West Germans were stranded in Berlin and are being flown home.

have leaked from sacks and corroded aircraft controls, it was put into baskets which were then slung outside the fuselages.

For West Berliners, all commodities were strictly rationed. The authorities ordered severe cuts in electricity to save 600 tons of coal, out of a daily consumption of 1,600 tons. There were no subway trains or trams at night, when the city was virtually blacked out with 75 per cent of street lights switched off. Petrol was rationed to 5 gallons a month to each motorist. Unemployment rose as industry was hit by the fuel cuts and shortages of raw materials.

The Soviet intention had been to force the Western Allies out of Berlin by mid-August, but summer turned into autumn with no change in the confrontation. Marshal Sokolovsky, the Soviet military governor, was told by Moscow that in no circumstances was he to undertake further negotiations with the British and Americans, and nothing was to interfere with the strategy of undermining their morale.

There was severe hardship for West Berliners in the ensuing winter but they survived, determined to support the Western resistance and never to surrender to the Soviet siege. They knew that, across in the Soviet sector, East

Berliners at mealtime during the blockade. Electricity, like all other commodities, was severely rationed and power cuts were frequent.

German communists were forming a 'shadow government' ready to fill the vacuum if the three Western Allies should abandon the city.

Protests and accusations flashed between Moscow and the Western capitals with no sign that either side would yield. It was not until the late spring of 1949 that Moscow finally realized that there was no chance that the Allies would quit Berlin. The airlift, patently a huge success, won the admiration of the Western world and the courage, endurance and resolve of West Berliners remained unshakeable.

After prolonged negotiations at the United Nations headquarters in New York, Russia agreed to lift the blockade and set one condition: a meeting of the foreign

None of the talks held throughout the blockade reached a satisfactory conclusion. Here, a Four-Power meeting of economic and transport chiefs is in progress in Berlin.

ministers of Britain, the US, France and Russia to discuss German reunification. They did, indeed, meet in Paris from 23 May to 20 June 1949 and the talks, like those held throughout the blockade, ended in deadlock. The defeat suffered by the Russians was a humiliation, and a great moral victory to the Allies. It seemed the reunification of Germany was now not even negotiable.

But the blockade was over. It ended on 12 May 1949 and traffic on land, along the canals and in the air, resumed its normal movement after an interruption of 322 days. Sixty thousand airmen had taken part in the airlift in which British and American aircraft made 195,530 flights carrying over a million tons of freight. It was a triumph for the Western Allies that reinforced their resolve to defend their democratic rights in Berlin and never to abandon the city now irrevocably divided, politically and economically.

Jubilant crowds cheer the first British truck across the border on the lifting of the blockade on 12 May, 1949.

4
Uprising

East Berliners buying fruit in West Berlin, where food shortages were rare and the market price remained stable.

In the years following the blockade, the differences between life in East and West Berlin became more obvious. While West Berliners enjoyed prosperity and high wages, East Berliners struggled to make ends meet under the severity of the communist system and a badly flagging economy.

The first uprising against the communist regime was crushed on the streets of East Berlin by thousands of Russian troops supported by tanks, armoured cars and artillery. It happened on 17 June 1953, a date revered today by Germans longing for the day when their divided land will be re-united. The dream, however, is still as far from reality as it was on that fateful day when Russian bullets ended a brief but memorable revolution.

The attempt to unseat the communist government of East Germany was the climax of unrest in major industrial centres, caused by persistent severe rationing, hardship and persecution and, finally, a decree issued by the East German government ordering workers to step up production or suffer a pay cut.

Two thousand East Berlin building workers engaged on a show housing project, known as 'Stalin Allee', led the demonstrations, which began on June 16, specifically against the order issued the previous month demanding 10 per cent more output – 'or 10 per cent less pay'.

The bricklayers' march on government offices was joined by factory workers and housewives. For three hours they shouted down government ministers trying to pacify them. There were demands for the resignations of Otto Grotewohl, the prime minister, and his deputy, Walter Ulbricht. The demonstrators called for free democratic elections and 'an end to slavery'.

Government ministers were summoned to an emergency meeting while the crowds continued to shout their demands. Loudspeaker vans then approached the people and announced that the decree for increased output had been cancelled. But this did little to appease the angry thousands, who carried on roaming the streets, shouting

A mass demonstration of East German workers, held to protest against food shortages and the government demand for increased production.

protests, and promising more demonstrations the next day. The police had been kept off the streets. The East German authorities had recognized that to challenge the crowds would have meant bloodshed.

But the next day the mood had changed noticeably. Russian troops had been brought in and the tension heightened. Tanks and field guns were positioned at key points in East Berlin. Faced with a worsening situation, the Soviet military authorities had taken command and declared martial law.

Early in the morning, the atmosphere was comparatively calm. Russian soldiers in full battle equipment were stationed at the Brandenburg Gate leading to the Unter den Linden, East Berlin's most famous thoroughfare. A young man climbed to the top of the Gate and, ignored by the soldiers, tore down the red flag that had flown there since the city fell to the Russians in 1945. When he reached the ground, the gathering crowd of demonstrators showered him with flowers and cigarettes. Then they ripped the flag apart.

A Soviet tank and troops on patrol on the streets of East Berlin after the riots.

By 11 am, the crowd had grown to more than 100,000 and was marching towards government buildings in the Wilhelmstrasse and Leipzigerstrasse. They faced Russian tanks, troop carriers and field guns.

Suddenly, the tanks went into action, driving at high speed around the Marx-Engels Platz and chasing off many demonstrators. But the main body of the procession marched on, with hundreds of East German police unable to stop them. Twenty policemen were pushed aside and trampled by the marchers.

Then a Russian T-34 tank, towering above the crowds, roared onto a pavement followed by five others, and scattered the mob. Many people hid from pursuing tanks in a nearby tangle of bombed buildings and half-cleared sites. They shouted to the crews in the tank turrets, 'Go home to Moscow'.

Uniformed and plain-clothes police made several arrests, dragging off their victims and beating them with truncheons. By now a full-scale riot had developed. Buildings were burning, propaganda hoardings along the streets were set on fire and a police barracks went up in flames. Red flags were pulled down and destroyed.

Crowds on the streets of East Berlin watching a burning coach.

The rioters advanced towards a line of police sheltering beside four Russian tanks. They launched a hail of paving stones at them, some clanging against the sides of the tanks. Warning shots were fired by the police and the crowds scattered, then re-formed with cries of: 'We will march on. "The Ivans" won't fire at us. The People's police are cowards'.

In the Unter den Linden, Russian tanks were pelted with stones and some youths tried to climb on to them and dismantle their wireless masts. This time, warning shots came from the tanks and the rioters ran for cover.

As the riots grew in intensity, Russian troops and East German police opened fire at the crowds. There were hundreds of casualties, including a small number of dead. One rioter was crushed to death by a tank. Bursts of gunfire even reached West Berlin, wounding sightseers gathered on the border.

The riots continued into the evening, but by midnight, East Berlin was quiet under a curfew. The Russian commandant, Major General Dibrowa, who took over from the paralysed East German government, proclaimed a state of emergency. A statement signed by Prime Minister Grotewohl said the riots had been caused by 'provocateurs and Fascist agents of foreign powers'.

Further riots and demonstrations took place throughout East Germany. Here, a Soviet tank on the streets of Leipzig attempts to quieten the rioters.

At the burial service for the 7 victims of the riots in East Berlin, the West German chancellor, Dr Adenauer, swore to free all Germans trapped behind the Iron Curtain.

By the following morning, as 12,000 Russian troops with about 260 tanks occupied East Berlin, there were reports of violent demonstrations from Magdeburg, Chemnitz, Leipzig, Dresden, Rostock and other major East German towns. In Magdeburg, Russian tanks opened fire on a crowd of 10,000, which had stormed a prison where political prisoners were held.

In East Berlin, Major General Dibrowa published a brief announcement that the first death sentence under martial law had been carried out against a demonstrator, described as a West Berliner working for a foreign intelligence service and 'an organizer of the bandits rioting against the State'. The execution brought an immediate, strongly worded protest from the three Allied commandants in West Berlin who described it as 'an act of brutality that would shock the world'.

Within a week, however, there were reports of more executions and arrests across East Germany as the hunt went on for the organizers of the revolt.

The uprising petered out under the harsh strictures of the Soviet authorities in East Berlin and achieved little, apart from revealing the sense of bitterness and frustration that existed throughout the country against the communist regime. But the decree demanding higher industrial output was never reimposed and church leaders arrested during a campaign of persecution earlier in the year were freed.

The East German government remained shocked by the events of the summer and were left to watch the tide of refugees to the West increasing every month.

5
The Berlin Wall

By 1961, Russia was becoming highly alarmed at the continuous wave of refugees leaving East Germany. The country was fighting a losing battle to rebuild its shattered economy and, with the loss of so much of its workforce, it could not afford to be weakened any further. In the summer months, 20,000 a day were crossing the border into West Germany. In the previous year, 200,000 East Germans had crossed over, most of them in Berlin. By now, the exodus required a drastic remedy.

In 1958, the East German leader, Walter Ulbricht, had approached the Soviet authorities to request that they take over West Berlin and so stop the flow of emigrants. Khruschev, the Soviet premier, agreed to this and delivered an

Refugees in a reception hall. The constant flow of East Germans to the West was bleeding the country's economy white.

ultimatum to the Western Allies. He proposed that the three Western powers should leave Berlin within six months, and that access to the city, including the air corridors, should be controlled by the East German government. But the Western allies refused to budge and, a year later, Khruschev withdrew his demand. But the supreme question remained of how to stop the refugees.

In June 1961, there were rumours in Berlin that the East German government would divide the city with a wall, which would act as a dam against the increasing numbers of refugees. The reports were promptly denied. Yet only two months later, when thousands of East Germans were pouring into West Berlin every day, the first steps were taken to transform the East German capital into a prison. In 1960, a desperate Ulbricht had approached the Russians once again with the plan to build a wall. They had agreed it was the only solution.

The first West Berliners to notice ominous signs on the night of 13 August 1961 were taxi-drivers who, from 2 am, were radioing their headquarters that the crossing points into East Berlin were being closed. By dawn, heavy lorries and cranes had rumbled up to the border and, from 6 am, barbed-wire coils were being strung out by East German soldiers. Guards from the Workers' Militia, a para-military organization recruited mainly from factories, appeared with machine guns before the startled eyes of West Berlin spectators. In 193 streets leading into West Berlin, the road surfaces were torn up, concrete piles slammed into the ground and trenches dug. At the same time, the fortifica-

The Soviet Communist Party leader, Khruschev, on a visit to East Berlin in 1957.

Armed troops between an astonished Berlin crowd and the barbed-wire barrier that preceded the Wall.

tions along the border with West Germany were being strengthened with more anti-personnel weaponry, such as mines, machine-gun posts, barbed-wire and searchlights.

Within a few days, amazed West Berliners saw the 3.5 metre high wall of concrete actually beginning to take shape. A work force of 50,000 East Germans were engaged in the operation and when the wall reached houses and buildings, the doorways were simply blocked off.

The wall grew into a bulwark 165 kilometres long, curling around the entire perimeter of West Berlin. It had 290 watch towers, 136 bunkers, 105 kilometres of trenches, 257 kilometres of dog runs, and 122 kilometres of fencing armed with warning devices. There were 14,000 border troops on guard day and night.

An East German soldier tries to calm agitated crowds as the Wall reaches waist-height.

Opposite *East German tanks stand guard as construction of the Wall progresses.*

41

Opposite *Victim of the Wall, Peter Fechter, who was shot and left to die by East Berlin guards, as he attempted to escape to the West.*

The Wall divided friends and families. This young couple in West Berlin have been cut off from close relatives in the Eastern sector.

Divided families on either side of the Wall could only communicate by waving from bedroom windows, or climbing lamp-posts to signal to each other over the formidable tangle of defences.

In the immediate years after the Wall was built, for thousands of freedom-seeking East Germans it was not impregnable. There have been 4,909 recorded escapes into West Berlin since 1961, and of those, 544 were made by border guards. Seventy-four East Germans died in attempts to scale the Wall and the number of wounded totalled 115. Over 3,000 escape attempts ended in failure and trial in the East Berlin courts.

West Berlin, however, will never forget the early years when so much blood was shed by so many would-be escapees. One of the worst incidents occurred on 17 August 1962 when Peter Fechter, aged eighteen, was badly wounded in a hail of bullets and left to bleed to death at the foot of the Wall because no one from East or West Berlin dared to help him.

In the 1960s, the wreaths were numerous along the pave-
ments of the Bernauerstrasse in West Berlin, where walled-
up houses formed part of the Wall itself. The flowers
marked the places were East Germans had jumped to their
deaths on the last lap of their flight to West Berlin. Many
others died trying to swim the River Spree.

Yet that stretch of water was also the scene of successful
escapes. Soon after the Wall was erected, the crew of a
passenger boat over-powered their captain, locked him in

44

his cabin and then took their families aboard. Under gunfire from East German guards they sailed the vessel across the river to freedom.

For two decades, the escape attempts continued undaunted, often undertaken with great ingenuity. Cars were turned into battering rams to crash through checkpoint barriers, tunnels were dug beneath the Wall, cables were strung over it from rooftops, and for those

The now barred escape tunnel through which an estimated 35 East Berliners escaped to the West.

In 1976, this family made their escape from East to West in the trunk of a car.

brave enough to face the border guards, bogus uniforms were tailored and documents forged. There is a museum in West Berlin today that pays silent tribute to the inventors of these daring schemes.

Today, West Berliners are accustomed to the Wall. The tensions first eased with arrangements, introduced in 1963, to allow East and West Germans to exchange visits. Over the years, the number of visits has increased, but although more people are able to move between East and West, the freedom to move is still restricted. To West Berliners, the Wall remains an implacable monument to communism and all it represents.

In East Germany, once the initial shock of the Wall had abated, the people stoically accepted their circumstances, and began with determination to build a future for themselves. Their efforts paid off, and by the 1970s, the average income per head in the GDR compared favourably with that of West Europe. Today, East Germans are mostly content with their lot, since the majority of them know nothing other than life under a communist system. However, the West undoubtedly still holds a great attraction for many.

6
The role of the troops

About 11,500 Allied soldiers, including 3,000 British troops, are stationed in West Berlin, to guarantee that the supreme power there remains with the military authorities and provide a protective shield for the Western enclave surrounded by communist territory.

The British sector in West Berlin is sandwiched between the French and American zones, and occupies the main commercial centre, including the Kurfürstendamm (the Oxford Street of Berlin), the Olympic stadium, which was

A British armoured car close to the Wall in the Potsdamer Platz area. Tours of the Wall are routinely carried out by all troops.

US Army soldiers on a raised platform check activity on the communist side of the Wall during a border patrol.

built in the 1930s, and a residential area. In the north-west, the 2,700 French troops are responsible for a group of pleasant suburbs set in countryside beside a lake, the Tegelsee, where rich West Germans sail their yachts. The 6,600 Americans are based in the poorer south-eastern industrial district of Kreuzberg where the most famous crossing point is found – Checkpoint Charlie. The former cultural heart of Berlin with the opera house,

theatres, museums and the fashionable Unter den Linden now comes under the jurisdiction of the East German government in East Berlin, with the support of East German and Soviet troops.

The duties of each of the Allied forces is similar. They all carry out regular border patrols and mount guard on the headquarters of the Allied Kommandantura. British and American planes also make routine flights along the length

The prisoner of Spandau, Rudolf Hess, is under guard by British, American, French and Soviet soldiers. For years, the question of his release on humanitarian grounds has been argued between East and West.

of the Wall.

The Western Allies and Soviet soldiers also share the task of guarding the sole inmate of West Berlin's Spandau Prison, Rudolf Hess, Hitler's former deputy and the last survivor of the Nazi elite, who is now in his nineties. It was on 10 May 1941 that Hess piloted a warplane from Germany across the North Sea on a mission to contact the British government. He parachuted to earth over Scotland and was captured and closely interrogated. The reason for his flight remains a mystery.

Hess remained under tight guard in Britain until the Nuremberg war crimes trials of Nazi leaders, held after the war ended. Hess was gaoled for life charged with crimes against peace and for plotting a war of aggression. Since then, his only contact with the outside world has been by letters and a visit once a month from a member of his family.

Hess provides a minimal task for the Allied soldiers in West Berlin. Their main duty still is, to ensure freedom of access to the city along the *autobahns* and waterways crossing East Germany, and through the air 'corridors' above communist territory. For the British, part of this operation involves manning the military train that makes daily trips to West Germany, 218 kilometres away. Except for Christmas Day and during the 1948–49 Berlin blockade crisis, this six-carriage train guarded by British troops and pulled by an East German diesel engine has run continuously from West Berlin to Braunschweig in West Germany. It is not used to carry military supplies – they are delivered to West Berlin by air – but operates as an important political demonstration of the Allied right of access to

In 1986, a US soldier observes events in East Berlin from his post at Checkpoint Charlie.

Soviet soldiers stand guard at the Soviet War Memorial in the British Sector of West Berlin. This is one example of Soviet presence in West Berlin.

West Berlin. The engine driver and guard may be East Germans, but under the post-war Four-Power agreements this unusual journey is strictly an Anglo-Soviet affair. The travel papers of the British troops are always inspected by a Soviet officer and clerk at Marienborn station near the West German frontier.

The parade of the Western Allies takes place in May, and in October the British and West Berliners join in a big tattoo featuring parachuting, motor cycling, horse riding and marching to military bands. In 1987, the Trooping of the Colours will be performed by the Gloucestershire Regiment before the Queen at her birthday parade in West Berlin. She is visiting the city for the 750th anniversary of its founding.

Few garrison towns in the world can match the friendly atmosphere built up over so many years between the Allied troops and the West Berliners, that provides such a genial contrast to the real reasons for the military presence in the divided city.

7
Espionage

On a freezing morning in February, 1986, Anatoly Shcharansky walked across Berlin's Glienicke Bridge to the West, after twelve years in Soviet prisons as one of Russia's leading dissidents.

Shcharansky, a small, delighted figure, was embraced by Mr Richard Burt, US ambassador in Bonn, who was in West Berlin to greet him. A convoy of cars took him to Tempelhof military airport where a plane was waiting to fly him to Frankfurt. In 1977 he was brought to trial in the Soviet Union on charges of spying for the US, and sentenced to thirteen years imprisonment. Shcharansky denied the accusations of espionage, and his wife campaigned in Western capitals for his release for more than a decade.

On the day of his release, the Soviet and American authorities exchanged five communist spies for three Western spies. The two groups passed each other over the bridge, the communists carrying heavy baggage and TV

Russian dissident, Anatoly Shcharansky, (centre) crossed the Glienicke bridge to freedom in February, 1986. For years his wife campaigned for his release from prison.

sets. The Western agents had few possessions with them. Shcharansky himself carried nothing: he even had to borrow a fur hat and coat.

Shcharansky had taken part in a spy swap. These exchanges between East and West have provided several chapters in the post-war history of Berlin. His plight, as he lingered for years in Soviet jails with worsening ill-health, was constantly reported in Western newspapers and on television. As a dissident he was a *cause célèbre*, representing all those prisoners of conscience suffering for

The famous Glienicke Bridge, where most exchanges between East and West have taken place.

their political beliefs in Iron Curtain prisons. The international campaign for his release finally reached the
agenda for the summit between President Reagan and Mr
Gorbachev, the Soviet leader, in Geneva in November,
1985. Shcharansky's release was, in fact, an important
feature of the diplomatic process in recent years to improve
relations between the super-powers.

Once it was decided that Shcharansky should be freed
in a spy swap, it was inevitable that the exchange should
take place in Berlin. The city split between East and

*US airman, Gary
Powers, whose US
spy-plane was shot
down over Russia in
1960. He was
exchanged for Soviet
spy Colonel Rudolf
Abel, in 1962.*

West has always been the background, both in fact and fiction, for this strangest of transactions between democracy and communism. In novels, Checkpoint Charlie and the Oberbaum footbridge across the River Spree have been the places where bartered secret agents have passed each other on their respective routes to their homelands. But more than once, imagination has been replaced by hard reality.

In real life, the Glienicke Bridge in the south-west corner of the US Sector was the setting for the exchange of the famous Soviet secret agent, Colonel Rudolf Abel and American pilot, Gary Powers, shot down over Russia on a spy-plane mission in 1960.

In 1964, at Heerstrasse, on the western edge of the British Sector, Greville Wynne, the British spy, crossed over from East Germany in exchange for Gordon Lonsdale, the Soviet agent.

These shadowy figures made headlines because they were the big pawns in the underground war of espionage. Many lesser agents have also been exchanged in the barter-dealing between East and West.

Greville Wynne, the British spy, spent 11 months in a Soviet prison before being exchanged in 1964.

The spies, the Wall, the city Sectors governed by Britain, France, America and Russia, and the underground and rail systems that ignore the barbed wire and watch towers on the surface, are all part of the jigsaw character of the world's most unusual city that presents an immediate contrast between life in the West and life behind the Iron Curtain.

Tourists flock to Berlin to see for themselves just what it is really like. After the warm, if brazen, atmosphere of West Berlin with its cafés, department stores and night clubs they probably experience an uneasy jolt when they mount one of the observation platforms and gaze across the Wall, to see East German border guards watching them through binoculars. It is not difficult to obtain a visa for 5 Deutschmarks to visit East Berlin and change more Deut-

schmarks into East German marks, set at an artificial rate of one-for-one. East Berlin is losing much of its drabness, although the Wall and its 'no-man's land' remain chillingly menacing. Many of the old buildings in East Berlin have been restored and visitors are urged, for instance, to visit the Pergamon Museum, named after a Greek altar it contains along with a reconstructed Roman market-place.

Tourists in the British sector queue for a chance to look over the Wall into East Berlin. This photo was taken in the 1960s.

59

But the city is unquestionably dominated by the Wall, which attained its twenty-fifth birthday in August, 1986. East Berliners commemorated the event with flags and a march by border troops, factory militia groups and a collection of army units. There were banners with the slogan: '1961–86: 25 years of the anti-fascist barrier'. A few hundred yards away in West Berlin, the Mayor, Herr Eberhard Diepgen, Herr Willy Brandt (SPD chairperson and mayor when the Wall was built), and the West German Chancellor, Herr Helmut Kohl, denounced the Wall and mourned its victims. They also stressed the need for increased contacts and exchanges across the Wall, for more detente and less Cold War.

Opposite *Erich Honecker, the East German leader, takes the salute at an East Berlin parade in 1986 to mark the 25th anniversary of the Wall.*

In West Berlin, demonstrations marked the 25th anniversary of the Wall. The banner reads 'The Wall divides one nation'.

A West Berliner
lights the torch on the
memorial stone
erected to the
reunification of
Germany, peace and
freedom. The
inscription reads
'Freedom, Justice,
Peace'.

8
The future

For more than four decades, Western statesmen have supported the idea of a reunited Germany. For West Germany, and not a few of their countrymen in East Germany, it is an ideal that can never be abandoned. But will Germany ever be united again? The argument is largely an academic one.

The reunification of Germany has been debated for years. Here, a West Berlin demonstration calls for reunion with the East following a Four-Power conference in 1954.

Erich Honecker spoke in terms of peace and greater communication between the superpowers, at the 25th anniversary of the Wall.

There is certainly no prospect that the West will reconcile its condemnation of the Wall and the border fortifications as barriers that enslave a nation, with the East German attitude that they are a defence against a fascist enemy. Herr Erich Honecker, the present East German leader, argues that the Wall has secured peace and cleared the path for detente between the super-powers. Without doubt, it ended the flight of hundreds of thousands of refugees to the West and saved East Germany from ruin.

Certainly Russia, whose losses numbered twenty million in the Second World War, would never accept the reunification of Germany, with all the dangers of another savage invasion of its country from the west. Russia demonstrated its iron determination to keep its East European empire intact and secure its frontiers, when it crushed the Hungarian uprising in 1956. The attempt by Alexander Dubcek, the Czechoslovakian leader, to introduce liberal reforms into his country in 1968 was also swiftly dealt with.

The 1956 Hungarian revolt was effectively quashed by Soviet military power. Here, anti-Soviet Hungarians burn the Red Flag.

The NATO meeting in Paris in 1954 in which West Germany was invited to become its fifteenth member country.

In 1954, when Cold War tension was high, Germany was invited to join NATO, the military alliance of the Western countries. It formally did so on 9 May 1955, and five days

LUXEMBOURG
NETHERLANDS
NORWAY
PORTUGAL
TURKEY
UNITED KINGDOM
UNITED STATES

later, on 14 May, the Soviet Union and the East European countries signed the Warsaw Pact, the communist counter alliance.

In 1976 the Helsinki Agreement, instigated by the Soviet Union, was signed by thirty-five nations. This guaranteed that the frontiers established in Europe at the Yalta and Potsdam meetings would remain fixed. It also eased Cold

East German guards remove a ladder used in a recent escape attempt. The graffiti on the West side of the Wall includes a huge peace sign.

War tension in Central Europe, though by no means completely. The West remained on its guard, unable to trust the Soviet Union particularly after the interventions in Hungary and Czechoslovakia.

The 1985 summit talks. President Reagan greets Soviet leader Mikhail Gorbachev.

To guarantee that the status quo in Germany is never changed, Russia has established in East Germany the largest and best equipped Soviet force outsides its borders. One of the most significant changes since the blockade of 1948 is that the Soviet Union now has its own nuclear force, and its military power is arguably as effective as that of the West. It seems improbable that either side would risk war for the sake of West Berlin, and with such a formidable armoury on both sides, the division of Berlin seems unlikely to change.

Recent East-West arms talks, however, have raised the prospect of moves to reduce the number of nuclear weapons based in Europe. A cut-back in the armouries of East and West, so long regarded as impossibly remote, would undoubtedly lead to other agreements to improve relations between the Eastern bloc and the Western nations. The divided city of Berlin would certainly be on the agenda of any international conference called to discuss solutions for world peace.

Date Chart

1941

10 May — Rudolf Hess, Hitler's deputy, flees to Britain.

1945

20 April — Soviet troops reach the outskirts of Berlin.

30 April — Hitler commits suicide.

2 May — Nazi troops surrender in Berlin.

8 May — VE day. Germany surrenders unconditionally to the Allied forces.

17 July — Churchill, Roosevelt and Stalin meet in Potsdam to implement decisions taken at Yalta conference on 11 February 1945 on the future of Germany.

1948

20 March — Russia quits Kommandatura, the Four-Power governing authority in Berlin.

22 June — Russia imposes blockade on Berlin.

26 June — US announces airlift to relieve Berlin.

1949

12 May — Russia lifts Berlin blockade.

23 May — Federal Republic of Germany formed.

7 October — German Democratic Republic declared.

1953

17 June — East Berlin uprising.

1956

3 November — Soviet troops crush the Hungarian uprising.

1961

13 August — The building of the Berlin Wall.

1962

26 June — Kennedy's 'Ich bin ein Berliner' speech.

1963 — 'Passierschein' regulations make cross-Wall visits possible for public holidays.

1968

21 August   Soviet troops crush Czechoslovakia's plan to 'liberalise' communism.

1972

3 June   Four-Power status in Berlin confirmed in Quadripartite Agreement.

1975

1 August   The Helsinki Agreement is signed.

1986

11 February   Anatoly Shcharansky freed.

13 August   25th anniversary of the Berlin Wall.

1987   750th anniversary of the city of Berlin.

Further reading

AMBROSE, STEPHEN E. AMBROSE *Rise to Globalism: American Foreign Policy since 1938* (Penguin, 1985)

COLLIER, RICHARD *Bridge Across the Sky: The Berlin Blockade and Airlift 1948–49* (Macmillan, 1978)

EINHORN, BARBARA *Living in Berlin* (Macdonald, 1986)

FOSTER, MARK ARNOLD *The Siege of Berlin* (Collins, 1979)

SHADRAKE, ALAN *The Yellow Pimpernel: Escape Stories of the Berlin Wall* (Hale, 1974)

SHEARS, DAVID *The Ugly Frontier* (Chatto and Windus, 1970)

WAGNER, ANGELIKA *Living in Berlin* (Wayland, 1980)

Glossary

Air corridors Arbitrary zones at fixed heights for aircraft traffic.

Allied Kommandantura The Four-Power supreme authority in Berlin.

Blockade To isolate an enemy, usually by troops or ships.

CDU Christian Democratic Union. The right-wing party of West Germany.

Cause célèbre A notable or famous trial or controversy, sometimes applied to the imprisonment of a dissident.

Cold War The state of political hostility and military tension between America and the Soviet Union.

Communism A classless society in which private ownership has been abolished and all things are owned by the community.

Containment America's policy of restraining communism in the post Second World War era.

Democracy A form of government in which supreme power is vested collectively in the people, and administered by them or by representatives elected by them.

Detente The easing of tensions between nations.

Dissident Term for rebels in communist countries who oppose communist doctrine on religious or other grounds.

FDP Free Democratic Party of West Germany.

FRG Federal Republic of Germany (West Germany).

GDR German Democratic Republic (East Germany).

Martial law Exercise of military powers in emergency situations.

NATO The North Atlantic Treaty Organization, a military alliance of 15 countries, established for their collective security.

SEP *Sozialistische Einheitspartei Deutschlands* Socialist Unity Party (Communist Party of East Germany).

SPD Social Democratic Party of West Germany.

Truman Doctrine America's policy, announced by President Truman, to supply political, economic and military aid to any country threatened by foreign pressure or invasion.

Index

Picture Acknowledgements

The publishers would like to thank the following for the loan of their photographs in this book: Camera Press 9, 14, 15, 23, 29, 40, 43, 47, 53, 56, 58, 64, 65. Daily Telegraph Colour Library COVER. Robert Hunt Library 8, 10, 11, 17, 18, 21, 24, 26, 38. Popperfoto FRONTISPIECE, 12, 16, 19, 22, 25, 27, 28, 30, 31, 32, 33, 34, 35, 36, 37, 39, 41, 42, 44, 45, 46, 50, 51, 54, 57, 59, 60, 61, 62, 63, 68, 70. The Research House 48, 52, 66. Wayland Picture Library 20. The map on p. 13 was drawn by Malcolm Walker.

ANIMALS
ON
THE EDGE
ELEPHANT

ANIMALS
ON
THE EDGE
ELEPHANT

by Anna Claybourne

BLOOMSBURY

LONDON BERLIN NEW YORK SYDNEY

Published 2012 by
Bloomsbury Publishing Plc
50 Bedford Square, London, WC1B 3DP

www.bloomsbury.com

ISBN HB 978-1-4081-4827-3
ISBN PB 978-1-4081-4958-4

Picture acknowledgements:
Cover: Shutterstock
Insides: All Shutterstock except for the following; p7 bottom left ©Thomas Breuer via
Wikimedia Commons, p14 bottom right ©ZSL, p15 top ©ZSL, p15 ©William Gordon
Davis/ZSL, p18 ©James Godwin/ZSL, p19 centre left ©James Godwin/ZSL, p19 top and
centre right ©ZSL, p21 centre left ©Hannah Thompson/ZSL, p21 centre right ©ZSL, p23
both images ©ZSL, p27 top inset ©ZSL, p30 bottom ©ZSL/ECN, p31 both images ©ZSL/
ECN, p34 bottom left ©ZSL/ECN, p35 middle left ©ZSL/ECN, p39 all images ©ZSL, p41
bottom right ©Hannah Thompson/ZSL

Manufactured and supplied under licence from the Zoological Society of London.

Produced for Bloomsbury Publishing Plc by Geoff Ward.

A CIP catalogue for this book is available from the British Library.

Printed in China by C&C Offset Printing Co.

CONTENTS

MEET THE ELEPHANT

There's no mistaking an elephant. With its long, twisting trunk and giant flapping ears, it looks like no other creature in the world. And of course, it's also the biggest animal that lives on land.

How big?

REALLY big! A large **bull** (male) African elephant can be 7m long and almost 4m tall – bigger than most classrooms. He has a trunk and tusks up to 2m long – more than a man's height – and ears the size of a double bed. If you put him on a giant set of weighing scales, you'd have to put 200 ten-year-olds on the other side to make it balance!

DID YOU KNOW?

- Elephants cannot jump
- An elephant can run at 40km/h – faster than most humans
- There are 40,000 muscles in an elephant's trunk
- Elephants are good swimmers
- Elephants can sleep standing up

The **African savannah elephant** is the biggest elephant. It lives in grasslands, forests, **scrub** and farmland across most of Africa.

What are elephants like?

Elephants are plant-eaters, and mostly live in small groups. They are very strong and intelligent. They are found in Africa and Asia, and there are two different **species**, and one elephant **subspecies** or type.

Elephants in trouble

There aren't nearly as many elephants as there used to be. Experts think that about 500,000 African savannah elephants live in the wild, and their numbers have now started to go up again. But Asian elephants are much more **rare**. There may be only about 30,000 of them left. There is a lot of **conservation** work going on to help elephants survive. You can read more about it later in this book.

The **Asian elephant** has a rounder head and smaller ears than African elephants, and females don't have tusks. It lives mainly in forests in south-east Asia, from India to Indonesia.

The **African forest elephant** is closely related to the African savannah elephant. It lives in the forests of Central and West Africa.

FACT FILE: LATIN NAMES

Like all living things, each elephant species has its own special scientific name, written in Latin.

African elephant	*Loxodonta africana*
Forest elephant	*Loxodonta cyclotis*
Asian elephant	*Elephas maximus*

African savannah elephant   Human

ELEPHANTS ON THE EDGE

Like many wild animals, elephants are in trouble – and it's mainly because of human activities. Sadly, people have hunted and harmed millions of elephants.

Problems for elephants

There are usually lots of reasons why a species becomes rare and at risk. This is especially true with elephants. They have been hunted for sport, for their skin and meat – and most of all, for their tusks, which are used as **ivory**. They are killed to protect farms and villages from them. In the past, a lot of elephants were also captured to be used as working animals. Elephants have also suffered from **habitat loss**. This happens when people take over their **habitats** – the wild places where they live – to make farmland, roads or towns.

Endangered species

An organisation called the **IUCN**, short for International Union for Conservation of Nature, keeps lists of animals that are in danger of **extinction** in the wild. The Asian elephant is listed as **endangered**. This means it is at risk of dying out.

African elephants are listed as **vulnerable**, which is almost as serious as "endangered". Experts aren't sure how many African forest elephants there are left – but they think they are endangered too.

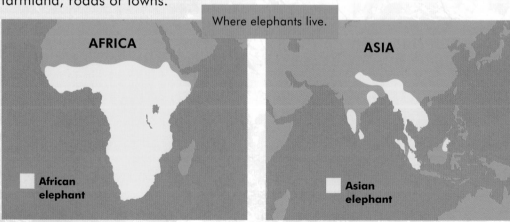

Where elephants live.

AFRICA

ASIA

African elephant

Asian elephant

Edge of existence

The Asian elephant is also listed by the **EDGE** of Existence programme as an EDGE species. That means it is not only endangered, but unusual and has few relatives. If animals like this die out, there will be nothing like them left. **ZSL**, the Zoological Society of London, runs the EDGE programme and is working on conservation projects to help the Asian elephant.

THE ASIAN ELEPHANT

Why is the Asian elephant more at risk? One big reason is that Asian countries often have bigger human **populations** than African countries. Lots more people live there, and they need more space for farmland and homes. So elephants have only been left with small patches of wild land here and there.

A road now cuts through the forest in Thailand where these Asian elephants live.

THE ELEPHANT'S COUSINS

Elephants aren't closely related to other large land animals, like hippos and rhinos. Instead, their closest relatives are water animals called manatees and dugongs, and the hyrax, a much smaller animal. Other types of elephants, such as the woolly mammoth, are now extinct.

Hyraxes look more like guinea pigs than elephants, but they are elephants' closest living relatives.

ELEPHANTS IN THE WILD

In the wild, you won't usually see just one elephant, but a herd. Elephants are **very** sociable – especially female elephants. They like to live in groups and look after each other.

Family groups

An elephant herd is made up of about 10 elephants. They are all either adult **cows** (females), or **calves** (babies). The leader is usually an older female, called the **matriarch**. The others in the herd are her own babies, her grown-up daughters, and *their* babies. So the matriarch is really a grandma who is in charge of the family. Male elephants can live alone, or get together in small groups.

Elephants keep growing as they get older, so the old matriarch or grandma is usually the biggest in the herd.

LONG-DISTANCE CALLS

Elephants can tell what's happening a long way away, by detecting **vibrations** that travel through the ground. They can sense a thunderstorm that will bring rain, a **stampede** of animals that might mean danger, or low, rumbling noises made by other elephants.

Safety in numbers

Adult elephants are too big for other animals to hunt, but lions do sometimes hunt elephant calves. So all the elephants in the herd help to protect the babies. At night, or if there's a **predator** around, the adults form a circle around the calves, to keep them safe.

On the move

Elephants need to eat for most of the day. They have a large home **range**, or area, and wander around it to find food and water. An elephant herd can spend 16 hours each day moving around and feeding. In that time, they can walk up to 80km. However, they never wander too far from a river or **watering hole**, as they need a nice big drink of water at least once a day.

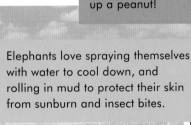

An elephant's trunk has many uses. It's so strong it can pick up a huge log, yet the tip is so delicate, it can pick up a peanut!

Elephants love spraying themselves with water to cool down, and rolling in mud to protect their skin from sunburn and insect bites.

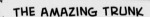

THE AMAZING TRUNK

An elephant's trunk is incredibly useful. Elephants use their trunks to:

- Suck up water to drink
- Suck up water to shower with
- Breathe through, and use as a snorkel when underwater
- Smell food, danger, and other elephants
- Make a loud trumpeting sound
- Push things over
- Pick up heavy objects
- Pick up small objects using the finger-like tip of the trunk
- Cuddle, stroke or hold on to other elephants
- To reach for food that is high up like mangos
- To pull down food like branches and bamboo

ELEPHANTS AND US

Since ancient times, especially in India and Thailand, humans have kept elephants as pets, trained them to do useful jobs, and even worshipped them as holy animals.

Working elephants

As the elephant is so big and powerful, it used to be seen as a suitable animal for a king. Famous rulers might ride an elephant in a royal ceremony or procession, or even into battle. Elephants can do other, less glamorous work too, such as **logging**. Instead of people cutting down trees, they can train elephants to push them over and carry the logs to where they are needed.

A brain for learning

Elephants are clever. They can learn how to follow lots of different instructions, using different commands and signals. Traditionally, elephants were trained from a young age, and each elephant had its own trainer and keeper, called a **mahout**. This still happens, to train elephants for forest work, or for riding, but it's much less common than it used to be.

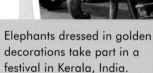

Elephants dressed in golden decorations take part in a festival in Kerala, India.

ELEPHANTS AT WAR

Elephants were used as war animals for thousands of years. Most working elephants are female, but males were used in war because they are more **aggressive**. War elephants looked scary, could charge and trample enemy armies, and give their riders a safe height and a good view.

Is it cruel?

Some of the methods used to train elephants can be cruel, and some working elephants get injured and worn out. There are elephant rescue centres for working elephants that have been mistreated, and campaigns against cruel training methods. However, elephants can also learn by being given rewards, instead of being treated harshly.

Many cultures have elephant gods, legends or beliefs. This is Ganesha, the elephant-headed god of new beginnings, in the Hindu religion.

DO ELEPHANTS EVER FORGET?

A famous saying about elephants claims, "Elephants never forget!" and it seems there really is some truth in it. Elephants can often recognise other elephants or zookeepers when they meet them, even after years apart. Wild elephants also seem to remember when humans have harmed them. Their ability to learn also shows that they have a good memory.

A working elephant carrying branches, with its trainer riding on top.

ELEPHANTS IN ZOOS

Around the world, there are about 2,000 elephants living in zoos. They are very popular with visitors.

What do elephants need?

Elephants need space, so their zoo **enclosures** have to be big. They also like natural surroundings like grass, pools to bathe in, and trees and rocks to rub against. Although elephants come from Africa and Asia, they don't mind cool temperatures – but they do need an indoor area where they can shelter from storms, or enjoy some privacy if they want to.

Booooored!

As elephants are intelligent, they can get bored. Zoos have to provide ways to keep them interested and entertained. They hide food for the elephants to find, and give them wooden poles to push and scratch against. Some elephants enjoy playing with toys, like swinging tyres or bouncy balls.

A baby elephant at ZSL Whipsnade Zoo gets to grips with a rubber tyre.

Elephants are very strong, so their enclosures need super-strong fences or walls that they can't break through.

ZSL Whipsnade Zoo's herd of Asian elephants go for a walk, holding onto each other tightly!

Jumbo carried several people at a time on his back.

Who's in the zoo?

All three species of elephants can live in zoos. But Asian elephants are the most common, as they're smaller and easier to look after. Also, as they are endangered, zoos keep them to study them and try to help them survive.

Emotional elephants

Elephants are happier if they can be close to other elephants. Most zoos try to recreate a natural elephant herd, so that female elephants can be with their family members, and spend time together. Male elephants are harder to look after, as they sometimes enter a bad-tempered, violent state called **musth**, when they can be very dangerous.

JUMBO

Jumbo, an African bull elephant, was one of the best-known zoo elephants ever. He was born in Sudan, Africa, and taken to a zoo in Paris, then to London Zoo in 1865. He was very popular with visitors, and famous for giving children rides. The name Jumbo came from the African word "Jambo" meaning "hello". Because of Jumbo the elephant, the word "jumbo" is now used to mean "enormous".

WHAT ELEPHANTS EAT

Elephants eat plants. Which plants, and which parts of them, depends on the elephant and where it lives. Whatever they eat, elephants need a massive amount of it every day.

How much?

An adult elephant gobbles up between 150 and 300kg of plant based food per day, the same weight as about 1,000 apples! African savannah elephants eat more grasses and leaves, while Asian and forest elephants find more fruit. But all elephants can eat grass, leaves, roots, fruits, plant stalks, **shoots**, nuts, seeds, and even tree bark. On top of that, an elephant drinks up to 250 litres of water each day, enough to fill a bathtub right to the top.

In the zoo

In the zoo, keepers feed the elephants on hay, leafy branches called **browse**, and fruit and veg such as bananas, apples, pears, cabbage and carrots. They also have **herbivore pellets**, a special food designed for plant-eaters.

As elephants eat for most of the day, they need food all the time. To make it more exciting for them, the keepers spread the food around different parts of the enclosure for them to find. Sometimes they put it on high platforms, or hide it in special feeders that have lots of holes and cracks for the elephants to reach their trunks into.

A zoo elephant reaches up to collect a mouthful of hay from a dangling hay feeder.

Elephant buns

In old songs and stories, zoo elephants eat buns and cakes. Long ago this was true – visitors could buy buns and feed them to the elephants. Today, they don't have buns very often, because they are bad for their teeth. But elephants still love buns, so they might get one on their birthday or at Christmas!

To drink, elephants suck water into their trunks, then squirt it into their mouths.

ELEPHANT FOOD SHOPPING LIST

At most zoos, the elephant food shopping list looks like this:

Hay
Carrots
Oranges
Pears
Herbivore pellets

Bananas
Cabbages
Apples
Maize
Fruit tree branches

ELEPHANT POO

After eating so much food, a typical elephant makes a LOT of poo, or **dung** – enough to fill a big wheelbarrow each day. In the wild, it's a useful **fertilizer**, making the soil better for plants to grow in. It also provides food for some animals, such as the dung beetle.

This African elephant has picked up a big, tasty branch to munch on.

A DAY IN THE LIFE: ELEPHANT KEEPER

Elizabeth Becker is one of the elephant keepers at ZSL Whipsnade Zoo. She reveals what it's like working with elephants, and all the jobs that have to be done.

A day with the elephants

7:30am The first job of the day is to check the elephants are all OK, and give them their breakfast. While they're eating, we clean out their sleeping quarters.

8:30am Each elephant gets a bath and a scrub down using warm water and shampoo. We take this chance to check they're healthy, as well as clean! After this we let them out into the paddocks.

10.00am Time for one-to-one training for the younger elephants. Using a reward-based approach (that is, plenty of bananas!) we train our elephants to obey commands, such as lie down, go in a certain direction, and most important of all, STOP! This is essential for working safely with elephants.

Elephants love water, so getting a shower and scrub is one of their favourite parts of the day.

10:30am Tea break. The keepers have a break and talk elephants!

11.00am We spend two hours deep-cleaning the entire elephant barn. It's back-breaking work (have you seen how much poo an elephant produces?) – but only the best will do for our herd!

1.00pm Lunchtime for the keepers. We have a dining room in the elephant barn, so we're never far away from them. The walls are covered with our favourite elephant photos and newspaper stories.

The elephants at ZSL Whipsnade Zoo play in their paddock.

A keeper helps a baby elephant learn to lift his foot.

At ZSL Whipsnade the public can get a close look at the elephants when they go for their daily walk.

ELEPHANTASTIC!

At ZSL Whipsnade Zoo's Elephantastic! demonstrations, elephants and their keepers display their elephant training methods. Elephants show off skills like lifting their feet to be cleaned, lying down on command, or carrying branches with their trunks.

2.00pm After lunch we take the herd for a walk around the zoo, every day, come rain or shine. In summer, we finish it with the Elephantastic! demonstration. In winter, the herd get some extra time to munch on trees – to the dismay of the gardeners!

4.00pm Back at the barn, the elephants are given their dinner.

8.00pm One or two keepers come back to check the elephants and give them some supper. We always say goodnight to them too!

ELEPHANT CALVES

There are few animals cuter than a baby elephant.
But although they're cute, they're not that small.
Even a newborn elephant weighs about 100kg –
more than most humans – and stands up to 1m tall.

Meeting and mating

Male and female elephants usually live separately, in their own herds.
But to mate, a male and a female have to get together. They find each other by their **scent**, and by making loud mating calls. Young elephants take an unusually long time to grow into adults. They are finally ready to **breed** (have babies) when they are about 13 or 14.

This African elephant calf has started to grow its adult tusks.

BABY TUSKS

Just like us, baby elephants are born with "milk teeth". Their proper tusks only start to grow after the tiny "milk tusks" have fallen out, when the elephant is about two years old.

Having a baby

Elephants are also pregnant for longer than other animals. It takes almost two years for an elephant calf to grow inside its mother's body. When it is born, it feeds on its mother's milk, like other **mammals** such as dogs and humans.

There is almost always just one baby. Elephants do very occasionally have twins. But if this happens in the wild, usually only one of them survives, as the mother does not normally have enough milk for two.

FACT FILE:
HOW ELEPHANTS GROW UP

0-6 months: Feeds only on milk
6 months: Starts eating plants
5-10 years old: Stops feeding on milk.
13 or 14: Young male elephants leave the herd, while females stay and have their own calves or help to look after baby brothers or sisters.
Elephant lifespan: up to 70 years

When a calf is born, its trunk is small and not very strong.

NAMING GEORGE

In April 2010, Karishma, an Asian elephant at ZSL Whipsnade Zoo, gave birth to a new baby boy elephant. To raise money for elephant conservation, an auction was held to name the calf. The person who offered the most money was allowed to name him, and called him George.

Baby Asian elephant George shelters close to his mum, Karishma.

ONE ELEPHANT'S STORY: AZIZAH

Azizah is a female Asian elephant living at ZSL Whipsnade Zoo. She's had an eventful life, and has travelled halfway around the world to get to where she is today.

Born in the wild

Azizah was born a wild elephant in the forests of Malaysia, southeast Asia, in 1984. Unfortunately, as Azizah and her mother roamed around looking for food, they began to raid local farms for crops. They caused so much damage that they had to be moved.

When this happened, Azizah became separated from her mother, and was taken to Malaysia's Malaka Zoo. There she was known as Layang Layang, the name of a Malaysian island. She was hand-reared by the keepers, who fed her milk from a bottle.

This is the kind of wild forest habitat where Azizah was born, in her homeland of Thailand.

WHAT IS AZIZAH LIKE?

Azizah is usually a very calm elephant – but she has a tendency for star-gazing and is often found daydreaming. Her keepers think she's probably a genius elephant, and is pondering the wonders of the universe!

Azizah's journey

When she was two years old, the Malaysian government gave Layang Layang to ZSL London Zoo as a gift. In London, she got her new name, Azizah. For the next year, she continued to be bottle-fed. She settled in well at ZSL London Zoo, but in 2001, it was time to move home again! All of the elephants in London were moved to ZSL Whipsnade Zoo, which is a lot more spacious and better suited to large roaming animals like elephants.

Becoming a mum

Since then, Azizah has been an integral part of Whipsnade's elephant herd, and she has turned out to be a great breeder. She has had three calves: Euan, born in 2004, Donaldson, born in 2008, and her new baby, born in 2011.

Azizah with her herd, enjoying the autumn leaves at Whipsnade.

Azizah stands protectively over her tiny calf who was born in October 2011, after a pregnancy that lasted 700 days!

THREATS TO ELEPHANTS

These are some of the things that reduced numbers of elephants in the past, and can make it hard for them to survive today.

Elephant hunting

Long ago, people could hunt "big game" (large wild animals) as much as they liked. Many hunters took pride in killing the biggest animals they could – such as elephants! The elephants were then stuffed, or made into objects such as elephant's foot waste-paper bins.

An old illustration of a hunter taking aim at a herd of African elephants.

Elephant products

People also hunted elephants for their meat, skin, and ivory – the bone from the tusks. It was once used to make ornaments, knife and fork handles, piano keys, musical instruments, buttons and many other things. Ivory became less popular in the 1900s, when plastic was invented, and when people realised that using it harmed elephants. But some people still want it, so hunters still **poach** elephants – which means they hunt them even though it's against the law.

A bin made of an elephant's foot was a desirable household item in Victorian times.

ARE ELEPHANTS REALLY DANGEROUS?

Elephants are often seen as wise, calm, peaceful creatures. But an angry elephant can be seriously deadly, especially a male in musth, or a female who is protecting a calf. Elephants kill many people each year by trampling them or **goring** them with their tusks. This is one reason people who live near elephants sometimes try to get rid of them.

A big elephant charging towards you is a scary sight – and very dangerous!

Size matters

Because they are so big, elephants need a lot of space and food. If villages and farms start to take over their habitat, elephants end up competing for these things with humans. Being so big and strong, they can be deadly enemies. So people kill them to protect themselves, their homes and their crops.

Bits and pieces

Another problem is that roads, farms and villages break elephant habitat up into small areas. This is called **habitat fragmentation**. It means elephants can't roam around freely to find food, water or a mate.

WHAT ARE TUSKS?

Elephants' tusks are front teeth that grow incredibly long and strong. Elephants use them to dig for roots, chip bark off trees, and fight their enemies. Ivory made from tusks is very strong.

You can see these African elephants' tusks clearly as they play in a mud bath.

HELPING THE ELEPHANTS

Trying to help wild elephants is a tricky job. Local people aren't always keen to protect them, because they are dangerous and can cause damage. Working with elephants can be risky for scientists and conservation workers too. And for some poor people, poaching elephants might be the only way to make a living. But there are things we can do!

Saving habitats

Governments can make laws to ban logging, farming and building in wild elephant habitat, to save it from being destroyed.

A safe place to live

Elephants can live more safely in **national parks** and **wildlife reserves**, special protected areas that have wardens to guard the animals and catch poachers.

Stopping poaching

As well as banning elephant hunting, a worldwide ban on trading ivory has been agreed, so it is illegal to buy or sell it. Occasionally some **confiscated** ivory is still sold to raise money for conservation.

Tourists get close to a wild elephant on a safari trip.

A pile of African elephant tusks, ready to be sold for ivory.

Elephant attractions

One way to help endangered species is to make money from them being alive, instead of dead! National parks can become **ecotourism** attractions, where visitors pay to come and see elephants and other wildlife.

These tourists are being taken for an elephant ride, on trained Asian elephants.

This sign in Sri Lanka warns motorists to watch out for elephants, allowing them to move around more safely.

New jobs

Money from tourists pays local people to work as park managers, wardens or wildlife tour guides. Conservation schemes can also give local people jobs. This means there are fewer people logging, farming or poaching for a living.

Living together

Some conservation projects help people to live alongside elephants. They find ways to protect homes and crops, and give the elephants safe routes through their ranges.

Finding out more

Scientists need to find out as much as they can about elephants. The more we know, the easier it is to help elephants by protecting the right areas, and giving them the things they need most.

ELEPHANT STUDIES

We only know as much as we do about elephants because scientists have studied them carefully. They've tracked them in the wild, watched them closely in zoos, and even looked at elephants' insides. But there's still a lot more for them to find out.

Where are they?

To help elephants, we need to know where they live, how many of them there are, and how much space they use. Then we can pinpoint the best places to protect. Elephants aren't always easy to find, especially ones that live in forests. But scientists and researchers have other ways to **monitor** them, or keep track of them, such as counting their footprints and dung heaps, and the marks they leave on trees.

These elephants are gathering to suck water out of a hole they've found in the ground.

What are they doing?

Besides watching and counting elephants, scientists study what they get up to. They keep track of where, when and how elephants **raid** crops or villages, making maps of their movements. They can then work out the best places to put fences, or grow the most elephant-proof crops. They can even identify a particular elephant that is causing trouble. One solution for particularly troublesome elephants is to fit them with a radio collar that sends a text message to farmers when they get near to their fields.

Elephant-spotting

To get a good view of elephants, scientists sometimes wait near a lake or river, and count the elephants as they come to drink. In grassland areas, scientists spot elephants from the air, using a small aeroplane, **microlight** or hot air balloon.

In grasslands, such as this grassy plain in Kenya, Africa, elephants are easier to spot.

A fresh pile of elephant poo on a road in Zimbabwe, Africa.

WHOSE POO?

Working in zoos, scientists have found ways to tell from an elephant's droppings whether it's a female, and whether she is pregnant or could become pregnant. In the wild, they can use this to find out much more about wild elephants in an area, even without seeing them.

THE SALAK PRA PROJECT

Salak Pra is a wildlife sanctuary in Thailand, where around 150 Asian elephants live. ZSL helps to run a project there to find ways for the elephants to live safely side by side with farmers and villagers.

A wild place

Salak Pra is made up of wild forest habitat, but it is almost cut off from other wild areas by farms, towns and roads. The elephants naturally try to wander over a wider area, and sometimes raid nearby farms and villages for food. A large herd of elephants can munch up a whole field of maize or bananas in a few hours. Elephants have also been known to kill people, and people have killed them in revenge.

Maps and measurements

First of all, the conservation workers monitor the elephants' activities. They keep records of which fields and villages they visit, at what times of the year. They make maps of crop-raiding hotspots, and work out where the elephants are most likely to go at any one time. With this information, they can decide where to take action.

Elephants can cause a lot of damage to crops, even when they don't mean to. This coriander crop has been crushed by huge elephant feet.

Elephant repellents

Over time, studies at Salak Pra have found several safe ways to keep elephants away from precious crops:

- Watchtowers or platforms built high in trees let people look out for elephants, and scare them away before they can get into the fields.
- Elephants hate loud noises, so using a firecracker to make a loud bang scares them off.
- CDs hanging on strings, next to a lit torch, make a flashing effect that frightens elephants.
- Electric fences can work, but are expensive. Some farmers make fake electric fences that look like the real thing to the elephants.
- Farmers tie ropes around their fields and spread them with a stinky mixture of engine oil, chilli and tobacco. Elephants hate the smell.
- Switching to crops elephants don't like to eat, such as chilli plants and rubber trees, is a good way to get rid of them!

A farmer takes a turn on a lookout platform, watching out for elephants.

Shiny CDs, dangling in the breeze around a crop field, reflect flashes of light to scare elephants away.

ELEPHANT-SAVING SCHEMES

Lots of wildlife organisations are at work to help elephants. There are large and small schemes, in all the countries where elephants can be found.

African forest elephants

Like Asian elephants, African forest elephants live mainly in the jungle, where they can be hard to spot. Organisations are monitoring forest elephants in central Africa to find out how many there are and where they live.

Some areas of the forest elephant's habitat are destined to be cut down for timber. ZSL's Wildlife Wood project helps timber companies to do this without disturbing the elephants too much. They also leave some areas of wild forest for the wildlife, with smaller strips of forest, or **wildlife corridors**, linking them together.

An African forest elephant chews a mouthful of grass in its wild home.

HELPING THE FOREST

African forest elephants help the forest **ecosystem** – the habitat and other living things in it. They spread seeds around, bring down trees and fruits that other animals feed on, and make pathways that other animals use.

Finding hidden elephants

Conservation group Fauna & Flora International runs Asian elephant schemes in Cambodia, Indonesia and several other countries. They are studying remote, mysterious areas, such as the Dalai Plateau in Cambodia, to see if elephants live there.

Asian elephants often live deep inside thick forests, like this one in Thailand.

Elephant crossing

In some parts of India, elephants are often killed on roads, or by trains or electric power lines, as they try to move between different parts of their range. A wildlife charity called Elephant Family runs a project to create safe wildlife corridors to help them stay safe.

TOO MANY ELEPHANTS!

In Africa, schemes to help elephants, such as banning ivory hunting and setting up protected reserves, can have good results. In some places in East and Southern Africa, elephants are surviving and breeding so well that there are too many of them. They have to be caught and moved to other areas.

This sign in Thailand is warning people to watch out for elephants crossing the road.

ELEPHANT ENCOUNTER: TWINKLE TOES

The staff at Salak Pra in Thailand don't often see the elephants, as they are shy and hide in the forest. As elephants can be dangerous, it's not sensible to get too close. But sometimes, they do spot signs, such as footprints, that show an elephant has been close by. One example was an elephant the workers nicknamed Twinkle Toes, because he was so careful where he put his feet!

Baby trees

One of the projects in the area is a tree nursery, where villagers grow young trees until they are big enough to be planted in the forest. The aim is to repair damaged parts of the forest, making more habitats for wildlife. The tree nursery is right next to the forest.

An Asian elephant this size has to be incredibly careful to tiptoe around a plant nursery, without knocking anything over.

These footprints show where Twinkle Toes has been. Luckily, he didn't damage any trees.

Twinkle Toes breaks in!

One night, the electric fence surrounding the protected forest area broke down. So one of the elephants took his chance to go for a wander into uncharted territory. His footprints showed that he tiptoed into the tree nursery for a nose around, and wandered over to look at some tree saplings. Then he did a graceful three-point-turn, and ambled back to the forest.

All in order

When the nursery staff found the elephant's trail, they were amazed that he hadn't done more damage. Elephants are well-known for tearing down trees and smashing their way around – but Twinkle Toes was incredibly gentle and careful. It was lucky he was, too. He could easily have destroyed the whole nursery, which would have cost a lot of money to replace.

"I COULDN'T BELIEVE IT!"

Belinda Stewart-Cox, who runs the project at Salak Pra, said: "This elephant appears to have been deliberately careful not to damage anything. He lifted the back fencepost and laid it down, before making his way down an aisle of tree saplings only three feet wide. I was absolutely astonished."

Belinda Stewart-Cox, who works for ZSL with elephants in Thailand.

ELEPHANTS AT NIGHT

Elephants are active in the daytime, but they often go exploring or looking for food at night too – especially if there are humans around who they would rather avoid. Another elephant at Salak Pra, nicknamed Polite Tusker, sometimes wanders through the office buildings at night – also without causing any damage.

Even if an elephant is *very* quiet, signs like these can reveal where he's been!

SEE ELEPHANTS YOURSELF

For centuries, elephants have been used as a spectacle to draw crowds and make money. If they are poorly looked after, or treated with cruelty, they can suffer horribly. But it doesn't have to be like that! There are ways for you to see and admire happy elephants, while making sure your money is used to help them.

On safari

A safari used to mean a trip to Africa to hunt wild animals. Today, it means a trip to *watch* wild animals and take photos, not to harm them. You can go on a whole safari holiday, or just take a day trip, usually to a national park, where expert guides show you where and how to watch the wildlife safely.

Elephant sanctuaries

In many Asian countries like India, Thailand, Laos and Sri Lanka, there are elephant sanctuaries to care for retired, injured or orphaned elephants. They make money to care for the elephants by charging tourists to visit. Sometimes you can even feed them or watch them have a bath.

These tourists on safari are getting a great view of elephants at a watering hole.

Volunteering

Lots of elephant sanctuaries and national parks have schemes for **volunteers** to work at them for a couple of weeks, or even a few months. The volunteers pay for their visit, and help with jobs like cleaning up after the elephants, counting them or working in the park offices.

Baby Asian elephants at a sanctuary in Thailand get a snack of bananas!

AN ELEPHANT ENCOUNTER

Some zoos, including ZSL's London and Whipsnade, hold special sessions where you can meet elephants up close, or even spend a day as a zookeeper.

Camera crews and TV presenters often make documentaries in national parks, where they can get close to wildlife fairly safely.

A worker takes an elephant for a bath at an elephant orphanage in Malaysia.

GO TO THE ZOO

Seeing elephants in the wild might involve a big, expensive trip. If you don't want to go that far, you might be able to see real elephants at a zoo or wildlife park near where you live. (Check first, though, as not all zoos have elephants.) Some places to visit are listed on page 46.

CONSERVATION BREEDING

Conservation breeding **means helping animals in captivity,** such as in a zoo, to have babies. It can be a good way to help an endangered species increase in number. But does it work for elephants?

Breeding problems

Most elephants living in zoos are female, because male elephants are hard to look after. It's also hard work to move big bull elephants from one place to another, to match them up with females to breed.

On top of this, while some animals are good at breeding in captivity, elephants sometimes seem to find it harder to get pregnant.

DID YOU KNOW?

Most animals live longer in zoos than in the wild, because they are protected from natural predators. But many zoo elephants seem to have shorter lives than wild ones. This could change, now that most zoo elephants have much bigger and better enclosures.

These male and female African zoo elephants are getting ready to mate.

In this photo, Euan is still a calf, but getting quite big and grown-up!

This **ultrasound scan** shows another baby, George, growing inside his mother. Scans like these tell keepers if the unborn baby is healthy.

Can it be fixed?

No one knows exactly why elephants don't always breed as well in captivity as they do in the wild. Bigger, more open and natural-style enclosures are becoming more common, and this could help. Some zoos, such a ZSL Whipsnade Zoo, have had great success breeding Asian elephants.

Success story

Euan, an Asian elephant calf, was born in captivity at ZSL Whipsnade Zoo in 2004. As he would in the wild, he stayed with his mother, Azizah, and his herd for some years. In 2011, he was moved to La Reserva animal reserve in Seville, Spain. There, he might one day be able to breed.

ELEPHANTS ON FILE

Zoos that keep elephants work together to make a **studbook**, a list of all the elephants in captivity, who is related to who, and which couples have mated and had calves. This helps them plan which elephants to move and put into pairs. The studbook for Asian elephants in Europe is held at Rotterdam Zoo in the Netherlands.

A young Azizah makes some new friends at ZSL Whipsnade Zoo.

CAN WE SAVE THE ELEPHANT?

Will Asian elephants, or other types of elephants, become extinct? It's hard to be sure. The problems that threaten them have not gone away. There is still a lot of work that needs to be done to help them.

Stopping the slide

In some ways, the efforts we've made to help elephants have worked. As recently as the 1980s, all types of elephants were disappearing fast. Today, thanks to poaching laws, national parks and reserves, and conservation schemes, African savannah elephants are starting to recover. Maybe, with the right help, African forest elephants and Asian elephants will too.

People like elephants

Compared to some endangered animals, like toads, spiders or bats, elephants are quite lucky, because they are very popular. In many countries, attitudes have changed and now no one wants to buy ivory or other elephant parts.

People feel concern, respect and awe towards elephants. We love to see them in zoos, in national parks, and in the wild - but not in circuses and shows where they might be mistreated. Because of their popularity, people will pay to visit elephants and support elephant conservation.

There's no need to make piano keys from ivory - other materials work just as well.

Top of the heap

Luckily for elephants, they are usually not on the menu for other animals. When animals are endangered, being eaten by tigers, wolves or other predators can be the last straw. This doesn't happen to fully-grown elephants, as they are bigger than these predators, and more than a match for them. The biggest threat to adult elephants is actually humans.

Elephants used to be a common sight in the circus - today they are used much less.

HOW CAN YOU HELP?

- Visit elephants at the zoo – you'll learn more about them, and your fee will be used to help them.
- You, your family or your class could adopt an elephant.
- Go elephant-watching if you're on holiday where elephants live.

At Whipsnade and many other zoos, you could visit beautiful elephants like Karishma and her calf George, shown here.

ABOUT ZSL

The Zoological Society of London (ZSL) is a charity that provides conservation support for animals both in the UK and worldwide. We also run ZSL London Zoo and ZSL Whipsnade Zoo.

Our work in the wild extends to Asia, where our conservationists and scientists are working to protect elephants from extinction. These awe-inspiring animals are part of ZSL's EDGE of Existence programme, which is specially designed to focus on genetically distinct animals that are struggling for survival.

By buying this book, you have helped us raise money to continue our conservation work with elephants and other animals in need of protection. Thank you.

To find out more about ZSL and how you can become further involved with our work visit **zsl.org** and **zsl.org/edge**

African savannah elephants are currently surviving better in the wild than their Asian cousins.

ZSL
LIVING CONSERVATION

EDGE

ZSL
LONDON
ZOO

ZSL
WHIPSNADE
ZOO

Websites
Asian elephant at ZSL Whipsnade Zoo
www.zsl.org/elephants
Asian elephant at EDGE of Existence
www.zsl.org/edge
Adopt an elephant
www.zsl.org/adoptelephant
ZSL information on African forest
elephants
**www.zsl.org/conservation/
regions/africa/forest-elephant**
Elephant Conservation Network
www.ecn-thailand.org

Places to visit
ZSL Whipsnade Zoo
Dunstable, Bedfordshire, LU6 2LF, UK
www.zsl.org/whipsnade
0844 225 1826

Baby elephants are the key to future population growth, so helping elephants to breed is vital.

Elephants are happiest when they have plenty of space to roam and explore.

GLOSSARY

aggressive Easily annoyed or violent.

breed Mate and have babies.

browse Leafy branches used as food for animals.

bull A male elephant.

calf A baby elephant.

captivity Being kept in a zoo, wildlife park or garden.

confiscated To have something taken away by the authorities.

conservation Protecting nature and wildlife.

conservation breeding Breeding animals in zoos.

cow A female elephant.

dung Elephant poo.

ecosystem A habitat and the living things that are found in it.

ecotourism Visiting wild places as a tourist to see wildlife.

EDGE Short for Evolutionarily Distinct and Globally Endangered.

enclosure A secure pen, cage or other home or for a zoo animal.

endangered At risk of dying out and become extinct.

extinction To no longer exist as a species.

fertilizer Something that makes soil better for growing plants.

gore To stab with horns or tusks.

GPS Short for Global Positioning System, a way of finding where you are.

habitat The natural surroundings that a species lives in.

habitat fragmentation Breaking up natural habitat into small areas.

habitat loss Damaging or destroying habitat.

herbivore pellets Special food for pet or zoo herbivores, or plant-eaters.

IUCN Short for the International Union for Conservation of Nature.

ivory Material made from elephants' tusks, or other animal teeth.

logging Cutting down trees.

mahout Someone who looks after and trains an elephant.

mammal A kind of animal that feeds its babies on milk from its body.

microlight A very small, light aircraft.

monitor To check, measure or keep track of something.

musth A bad-tempered, violent state that male elephants go into.

national park A protected area of land where wildlife can live safely.

poaching Hunting animals that are protected by law and shouldn't be hunted.

population Number of people, or animals, in a particular place.

predator An animal that hunts and eats other animals.

raid To attack or steal.

range The area where an animal or species lives.

rare Very few and far between.

satellite An object orbiting the planet.

scent A special smell.

scrub A dry landscape with small, tough plants.

shoot The first growth of a plant from a seed.

sociable Friendly and happy to be with others.

species A particular type of living thing.

stampede Lots of animals running at once.

studbook A record of the animals of a particular species born in captivity.

subspecies A slightly different type of animal from the main species.

ultrasound scan A way of using sound waves to look inside the body.

vibrations Shaking movements.

volunteer Someone who offers to do a job without being paid.

vulnerable At risk, but not as seriously as an endangered species.

watering hole A pool where animals come to drink.

wildlife corridor A strip of natural habitat connecting wild areas.

wildlife reserve A protected area of land where wildlife can live safely.

ZSL Short for Zoological Society of London.

FIND OUT MORE

Books

Elephants Under Pressure by Kathy Allen, Fact Finders, 2010

100 Things You Should Know About Elephants by Camilla de la Bedoyere, Miles Kelly Publishing, 2007

The Elephant Scientist by Caitlin O'Connell, Houghton Mifflin Harcourt, 2011

Who Scoops Elephant Poo? Working at a Zoo by Margie Markarian, Raintree, 2010

What's it Like to be a... Zoo Keeper? by Elizabeth Dowen and Lisa Thompson, A&C Black 2010

Websites

Asian elephants at Chester Zoo
www.chesterzoo.org/animals/mammals/Elephants/asian-elephants

BBC Asian elephant information, videos and sounds
www.bbc.co.uk/nature/life/Asian_Elephant

Elephant webcams
www.animalcameras.com/elephants/live-elephant-webcams/

Places to visit

Chester Zoo
Upton-by-Chester,
Chester CH2 1LH, UK
www.chesterzoo.org
01244 380280

Twycross Zoo
Burton Road, Atherstone,
Warwickshire CV9 3PX, UK
www.twycrosszoo.org

Smithsonian National Zoo
3001 Connecticut Avenue NW,
Washington, DC 20008, USA
http://nationalzoo.si.edu/

San Diego Zoo
2920 Zoo Drive, Balboa Park,
San Diego, California, USA
www.sandiegozoo.org

Rotterdam Zoo
Blijdorplaan 8, 3041 JE Rotterdam,
The Netherlands
www.rotterdamzoo.nl

INDEX

OTHER TITLES IN THE ANIMALS ON THE EDGE SERIES

www.storiesfromthezoo.com

Penguin
ISBN: HB 978-1-4081-4822-8
PB 978-1-4081-4960-7

Rhino
ISBN: HB 978-1-4081-4823-5
PB 978-1-4081-4956-0

Tiger
ISBN: HB 978-1-4081-4824-2
PB 978-1-4081-4957-7

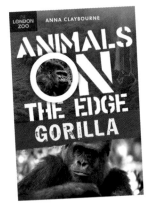

Gorilla
ISBN: HB 978-1-4081-4825-9
PB 978-1-4081-4959-1

Hippo
ISBN: HB 978-1-4081-4826-6
PB 978-1-4081-4961-4